Foundations – Faith Life Essentials
The Doctrine of Baptisms

© 2010 Derek Prince Ministries–International
This edition DPM-UK 2020

ISBN 978-1-78263-545-1
Product code: B104D

Scripture quotations are from the New King James Version of the Bible,
Thomas Nelson Publishers, Nashville, TN, © 1982.

This message is a transcript book with questions and study suggestions
added by the Derek Prince Ministries editorial team.

DPM

Derek Prince Ministries
www.derekprince.com

EXPANDED
VERSION:
GROUP
STUDY

The
Doctrine of
Baptisms

DPM

DEREK PRINCE MINISTRIES

Contents

About This Study Series

The Bible is God's Word and our "instruction manual" to find the path to salvation in Jesus. It then shows us how to walk with Him once we have come to know Him. Logically, therefore, it is a hugely important part of our challenge as Christian believers to study the Word of God.

A sad fact is that very often we forget most of what we have heard quite quickly! As a result, what we have heard often has little impact on the way that we continue to live.

That is why we developed these Study Guides. As Derek Prince has said numerous times in his teaching, "It is a general principle of educational psychology that children remember approximately 40 percent of what they hear; 60 percent of what they hear and see and 80 percent of what they hear, see and do."

This Study Guide is intended to help you to assimilate the truths that you have heard into both your head and into your heart so that they become more than just knowledge and will begin to change the way that you live.

Living the Christian life

This study is part of a series of 10 messages, based on the doctrinal foundation of the Christian life described in Hebrews 6:1-2 which says,

Therefore, leaving the discussion of the elementary principles of Christ, let us go on to perfection, not laying again the foundation of repentance from dead works and of faith

toward God, of the doctrine of baptisms, of laying on of hands, of resurrection of the dead, and of eternal judgment.

This mentions six specific foundation stones that we need to lay before we can build a dwelling place for the Lord in our hearts and lives:

1. Repentance from dead works
2. Faith towards God
3. The doctrine of baptisms – John's baptism, Christian baptism and baptism in the Holy Spirit
4. Laying on of hands
5. Resurrection of the dead
6. Eternal judgment.

When this teaching is applied in your life, with faith, we believe that it will deepen your relationship with God and enable you to live a truly successful Christian life.

How to Study

Each book contains a QR-code (or DVD) that links you to a talk by Derek Prince, the transcript of the talk and questions for personal application or to be discussed in a group setting.

Each video is about an hour long, divided in three parts. Set aside a reasonable length of time to read the Introduction, then watch or read Derek's teaching, and finally come back to the Study Guide to reflect on the Study Questions or to discuss them with your study group.

Once you have completed this series you will find that you have an excellent summary of the teaching. This will help you to share the content with others, whether to a friend, home group or congregation. The more you share the truths you are learning, the more they will become part of your own life and testimony.

Group Study

This study guide has been developed for use by small groups as well as by individuals.

Simply proceed through the material as a team, reflect on the questions and explore the statements together for a rich and rewarding experience.

Scripture to Memorize

In this book, we have chosen key Scriptures for memorization. They will relate in some way to your overall study. Memorizing them will place a spiritual sword in your hands which you, by the Holy Spirit, will be able to use in times of spiritual conflict.

The Word of God has supernatural power for those who will take the time and effort to "hide it in their hearts" by memorizing and meditating on it. As God's Word is hidden in your heart, it becomes constantly available to you for reference, comfort, correction and meditation. Put simply, it becomes part of your life.

Look up the verse in your own Bible and write it in the space provided. You will want to write and say this verse out loud several times until you are confident you know it well. Take time to meditate on the words and their application to your life. As a group, you could talk briefly about the meaning of the verse and its relevance to the lesson or share how you applied it.

You will be asked to recall your Memory Work at the end of the book.

The Doctrine of Baptisms – an Introduction

In the New Testament, three key baptisms are mentioned: the baptism of John, Christian baptism and baptism in the Holy Spirit. In this study Derek Prince will teach about the first two of these baptisms, both of which are baptisms in water.

Have you ever wondered where the word "baptism" comes from? Did you know that in each instance, a person is baptized "in" something and "into" something else? Did you realise that both Noah's ark and the Israelites, exodus from Egypt described in the Old Testament were types and shadows of New Testament baptisms?

You might have more personal questions about baptism in water, such as: Are there requirements that must be fulfilled before I make the decision to get baptized? How long should I wait before being baptised? Do I need to go to classes to qualify for baptism?

These are some of the many questions that Derek is going to answer for us from the Scriptures.

In this study, you will learn the significance of water baptism. Every time it takes place, water baptism is a fresh enactment of the death, burial and resurrection of Jesus Christ. In the early Church you could not become a full member of the Church unless you went through that enactment of the faith that you professed.

The spiritual significance of Christian baptism is three-fold: we are identified with Jesus in His death, burial and resurrection; as we are baptised, we die, we are buried and then raised again to a new life; we die to sin and become alive to Christ. We are baptised in water and into Christ.

Romans 6:4 tells us that, "We were buried with Him through baptism into death, that just as Christ was raised from the dead by the glory of the Father, even so we should walk in newness of life." In the old life before baptism we lived in fleshly ways, but the supernatural life that God gives us through the new birth requires supernatural power to live effectively and so gives us the promise of the Holy Spirit.

Read or watch now as Derek Prince takes you through this fascinating, extremely significant teaching on immersion in water.

Watch the Derek Prince video teaching *The Doctrine of Baptisms* on YouTube. Scan the QR-code or visit dpmuk.org/ foundations.

This video has been divided into three sections, following the chapters in this book. You will find the links to these sections when you tap the 'down arrow' to expand the information about the video.

SCRIPTURES TO MEMORIZE

Write down these verses and try to memorize them.

Romans 6:3

_____

_____

_____

_____

_____

Romans 6:4

_____

_____

_____

_____

_____

MEDITATION

A baptism is a transition—
out of an old way of life
and an old way of living
into a totally new way
of living.

The Doctrine
of Baptisms

This booklet is the fifth in a series of studies on the foundational doctrines of the Christian faith as they are enumerated in Hebrews 6:1–6. Previous to this study we have considered the first two of these doctrines in some detail: repentance from dead works and faith toward God.

In the previous study, *Faith and Works*, we considered the relationship of true faith and human works as it is presented in the New Testament. From our study we understood that faith in what God has done for us in Christ is the only means to true righteousness. Any effort on our part to earn or merit right standing with God by the works we do is a grave error which is soundly condemned in numerous places in the New Testament.

In our study we saw that there is a proper place for works: good works follow and proceed out of true faith. One of the first acts of obedience which should proceed from true faith is receiving water baptism, which we will consider in this study. Before we study the New Testament teaching on water baptism, however, we will consider the general teaching of the Scriptures on baptisms (plural) or "the doctrine of baptisms," which is the third of the foundational doctrines listed in Hebrews 6.

A baptism is a transition—out of an old way of life and an old way of living into a totally new way of living. It is a total immersion; all of our being is involved.

Let us look again at the Scripture passage we are studying:

> *Therefore, leaving the discussion of the elementary principles* [or basic truths] *of Christ, let us go on to perfection* [completion, maturity], *not laying again the foundation of repentance from dead works and of faith toward God, of the doctrine of baptisms, of laying on of hands, of resurrection of the dead, and of eternal judgment.*
> *Hebrews 6:1–2*

The "doctrine" of baptisms simply means "teaching about" baptisms. Notice that the word baptism is plural: baptisms. There are actually three different baptisms mentioned in the New Testament, each of which we will study in due course.

These baptisms are: number one, John's baptism, the baptism of John the Baptist; number two, Christian baptism, which is not the same as John's baptism; and number three, the baptism in the Holy Spirit. These are three distinct baptisms, all of which play an important part in the New Testament.

To Baptize—A Transition

The word baptize is not really an English word, but a Greek word written in English letters. Technically, it is a transliteration. The word is taken directly from the Greek word, baptizo, which is not translated but just written in English letters. There are various possibilities as to why this word was transliterated rather than being translated according to its true meaning. It may be just church tradition or it could be that the translators of the King James Version did not want to offend the Anglican Church by using the exact meaning of the word. I am not asserting any particular position.

However, if we go back to Greek, there is absolutely no question about the correct meaning of the word. It means "to immerse." It comes from a root word, bapto, which means "to dip."

Immersion can take place in one of two ways, and both of them are relevant to the New Testament. You can immerse something in water by putting it down into the water so that it is fully covered, or you can immerse something by pouring water over it. But whichever way you do it, it is total immersion, not partial. Therefore, when we think of a baptism in the New Testament, we must think of it as a total immersion.

Every kind of baptism spoken of in the New Testament represents a complete transition. We move out of one place into another. Our whole person moves, not just part of us. For that reason, I need to emphasize that baptism is total immersion. Our total being is affected by this process of baptism.

In or Into What?

The word baptism is used with two or three different prepositions which need to be explained. Baptize is used with the preposition in or into, or sometimes just to.

The preposition "in" refers to the element in which you are immersed. It may be water or it may be the Holy Spirit. When "into" is used, it describes the end product, or result, of being immersed. It is what we pass into as a result of the transition of baptism.

For instance, John the Baptist's baptism was in water into repentance, or forgiveness of sins. There is both an "in" and an "into."

The baptism in the Holy Spirit (which is covered in the book *Immersion in the Spirit*) is in the Spirit and into the body of Jesus Christ.

In considering baptism we need to ask these two questions: What is it *in*? And, what is it *into*?

To make this clearer, and to further clarify similarities among the different baptisms in the New Testament, we will refer to the following table. Note that each baptism—John's baptism, Christian (or water) baptism, and the baptism in the Holy Spirit—are each listed in the left-hand column. Across the top of the table are the requirements for receiving that baptism, the element in which the baptism takes place, and finally, the state or position into which one is baptized. The specifics of each baptism will be made clearer as we progress.

New Testament Baptisms

New Testament Baptisms			
Baptism	Requirements to receive	Element of baptism (IN)	New position or state (INTO)
John the Baptist	Repentance Confess sin Evidence of repentance	Water	Forgiveness of sins
Christian, or water	Hear the gospel Repent Believe Good conscience	Water	Christ Newness of life
Holy Spirit	Repent Be baptized Be thirsty Come to Jesus Ask Receive / drink Yield	Holy Spirit	Body of Christ

John's Baptism

John the Baptist got his name from the fact that he was the baptizer. We read in the gospel of Mark:

> As it is written in the Prophets: "Behold, I send My messenger before Your face, who will prepare Your way before You.
> The voice of one crying in the wilderness: 'Prepare the way of the Lord; make His paths straight.'" John came baptizing in the wilderness and preaching a baptism of repentance for [or into] the remission of sins.
> Mark 1:2–4

The ministry of John the Baptist was to go before the Messiah and prepare His way. His message was very simple. It could be summed up in one word: repent. Verse four should be translated, "into the remission of sins." People were being baptized with a baptism of repentance that led to the remission (or forgiveness) of their sins. Please note this in the table above: "Baptized in water," "into the forgiveness of sins."

The purpose of John's baptism was to prepare the way for the coming of Israel's long-awaited Messiah, Jesus of Nazareth. It is very significant that Jesus could not come—God would not release Him to come—until the hearts of God's people had been prepared by repentance.

I am inclined to think that the same is true of the coming again of Jesus. The hearts of God's people will have to be prepared by repentance. In some ways, repentance is the most crucial single message that God's people need today.

An Important Link

John's ministry was also a very important link between two different periods of God's dealings with His people, or two different dispensations. A "dispensation" is a given period of time in which God relates to His people according to certain principles that He Himself sets in place. John was a link between the dispensation of the Law and the Prophets, which began with Moses; and the dispensation of grace and the gospel, which came with Jesus. John is a crucial figure in the unfolding of God's whole purpose and he stands as a link between these two distinctly different periods of history.

Speaking about John in Matthew 11:13, Jesus says:

"For all the prophets and the law prophesied until John."

John the Baptist marked the end of the dispensation of the Law. As such, he was a transitional link to the new dispensation of the grace of the gospel. That makes him an important man. In a sense, he bisected the history of God's people. He ended one period and initiated another.

We know relatively little about John, and I have been inclined to underestimate the importance of his ministry. His ministry was brief, but it was crucial because it prepared the way for Jesus. His impact on the people of Israel was tremendous.

Then all the land of Judea, and those from Jerusalem, went out to him and were all baptized by him in the Jordan River, confessing their sins.
Mark 1:5

John's Impact

In a very brief period of time, John doubtless reached hundreds of thousands of people—the whole population of Jerusalem, Judea, and much of the surrounding area beyond. I often reflect on the unique way God does things. He does not hire a committee, rent a stadium, organize a choir and say, "Now we'll have a meeting." He accomplishes His purposes in the most improbable ways. In this case, He called just one man, dressed in a garment of camel's hair, who went out into the wilderness, and all the people went out to him. The people were brought out to John, not by organization, not by advertisement nor by publicity, but by the supernatural moving of God. That tends to be the way God does things—in an unexpected way.

We need the same today. Where the fire of God is burning, people will go. It doesn't matter what kind of a place it is. It doesn't matter what type of personality the preacher has or whether he is educated or uneducated. It only matters that God is there.

As far as we know, John the Baptist had no formal education, but he was a man set on fire by God. Jesus said later to the people of His day, "He was the burning and shining lamp [or light], and you were willing for a time to rejoice in his light" (John 5:35).

Unfortunately, those people to whom Jesus was speaking never caught the fire. They went to the light, they received the benefit of the light, but they never caught the fire. Jesus' commendation of John is very powerful: "He was a burning and a shining light." It is true scientifically that if you want to shine, you have to burn. There is no light without heat.

Let's take that to heart. If we are going to shine for Jesus, we have to burn. Let's pray that, wherever God puts us, we will be a burning and a shining light.

Requirements of John's Baptism

John's baptism required three actions on the part of the people who came to be baptized.

First, it was a baptism of repentance. Therefore, those desiring to receive his baptism needed to repent. Repentance, you will remember from our earlier studies, is not an emotion but a decision. It is coming to the end of something, turning around to face the opposite way, and going in the opposite direction. John demanded that those who came to him for baptism would meet that condition of repentance. It was, first, a decision, and then an action.

Second, John demanded the public confession of sins. This seems to have dropped out of the thinking of so many people in the Church today. I have learned by observation that it is extremely powerful when God's people are sufficiently convinced by the Holy Spirit to confess their sins. It has been the key that sparked various revivals in the past, especially the Welsh Revival in 1904, which was marked by people confessing their sins.

You do not necessarily have to confess your sins in public, but you do have to confess your sins. The only sins God is committed to forgive are the sins we confess. The disciple John says in his first epistle:

If we confess our sins, He is faithful and just to forgive us our sins and to cleanse us from all unrighteousness.
1 John 1:9

That sentence starts with a little word, "if." If we confess our sins. If we do not confess, we have no guarantee that God will forgive.

Many believers have a pile of unconfessed sin behind them. They come for healing or for a blessing and wonder why they do not receive it. They have a tremendous burden. David said his sins were "like a heavy burden" to him (Psalm 38:4).

Dear friend, you may be reading this with a heavy burden over you because you have piled up sins that you have not yet confessed. You would do well to get alone with God, open your heart to the Holy

Spirit and say, "God, show me what I need to confess." Remember, if you do not confess, you have no guarantee that God will forgive. If we confess, He will forgive.

The third demand of John the Baptist was evidence of a changed life. He required evidence that people had repented. When people came to him who apparently had not repented because they did not show the visible evidence of their repentance, John refused to baptize them (Matthew 3:8). In particular, those were the religious people of the day—the Pharisees and the Sadducees.

Jesus later pointed this out to the Pharisees, by saying, "Tax collectors [publicans] and harlots believed John and you didn't. They will go into the kingdom of heaven before you." (See Matthew 21:31–32.)

It is very hard for strongly religious people to come to grips with a new move of God. I often express it this way: when a new move comes in the Church, another story is added to the building. Then, generally speaking, those who are part of that move put the roof on what they believe God will do by saying, "This is it; no more." Then the next time the wind of God moves, the first thing He has to do is blow their roof off!

People who have identified with a particular move of God tend to be rather resentful and find it hard to move with what God desires to do next. This is just like the Pharisees, and John was a very plainspoken man when he confronted them about it.

People of Plain Speech

I once made a little study of the characteristics of people of whom the New Testament said, "They were full of the Holy Spirit." The first one mentioned was John the Baptist, who was filled with the Holy Spirit from his mother's womb. The others were Jesus, Peter, Paul, and Stephen. I made the rather frightening discovery that most of them ended their lives as martyrs.

I also discovered that they were all people of plain speech. They did not use nice, religious language. The Holy Spirit cannot endorse anything that is flimsy, muddled or unclear. He wants plain, clear speech. What John said a lot of preachers would never say today. For instance:

> But when [John] *saw many of the Pharisees and Sadducees coming to his baptism, he said to them, "Brood of vipers! Who warned you to flee from the wrath to come? Therefore, bear fruits worthy of repentance* [or answerable to a change of life], *and do not think to say to yourselves, 'We have Abraham as our father.' For I say to you that God is able to raise children to Abraham from these stones."*
> *Matthew 3:7–9*

That is an amazing statement! We cannot rely on our pedigree or on our background. We each have to meet God's conditions personally.

Those were the three requirements of John's baptism: repentance, public confession of sins, and evidence of a changed life.

I want to point out something else here, because it applies in every place where the word baptism is used. It says that John baptized them into repentance. (See "New Testament Baptisms" chart, page 10.) But, remember that he would not baptize them unless they had already repented. Baptism did not produce the repentance—it was the seal and evidence that they had already repented.

You will find this accurate in every place in which the phrase "baptized into" is used. It does not indicate that the baptism brought them in, but it is used to indicate that the baptism is the seal upon their entrance into that particular state or condition. We will look at this again later in this booklet.

Limitations of John's Baptism

The baptism of John only took people a certain distance, therefore it had certain limitations. First of all, it did not produce the new birth.

Jesus says of John the Baptist:

> *"Assuredly, I say to you, among those born of women there has not risen one greater than John the Baptist; but he who is least in the kingdom of heaven is greater than he."*
> *Matthew 11:11*

This indicates John was born "of women," but he was never born again in the New Testament sense. He did not enter into the new birth ["the kingdom of heaven"] because that was not possible until Jesus was resurrected. He was one of the greatest of those born of women, but he that is least in the kingdom of God is greater than John.

We are not greater because of what we are, but because of where God has put us in Christ. God has brought us into the kingdom through the new birth. Remember that Jesus said, "Unless one is born again, he cannot see [or enter] the kingdom of God" (John 3:3, 5). So, John had his God-given limitations.

Second (and this is very important), after Pentecost, the baptism of John was no longer accepted as valid. This is revealed in Acts 19.

> *And it happened, while Apollos was at Corinth, that Paul, having passed through the upper regions, came to Ephesus. And finding some disciples he said to them, "Did you receive the Holy Spirit when you believed?"*
> *Acts 19:1–2*

Notice that we are not told of what or of whom they were disciples. Apparently, Paul was not clear himself when he met them. Therefore, he asked a question which, I imagine, he asked everywhere he went: "Did you receive the Holy Spirit when you believed?" This proves that it is possible to believe without receiving the Holy Spirit.

Then Paul made a discovery:

They said to him, "We have not so much as heard whether there is a Holy Spirit." And he said to them, "Into what then were you baptized?" So they said, "Into John's baptism."
verses 2–3

There are different ways of understanding this. When they said, "We have not heard that there is a Holy Spirit," why did Paul say, "Into what then were you baptized?" Why did Paul use the word then? How is it possible they could have been disciples without hearing about the Holy Spirit?

One explanation is that Jesus told His disciples in Matthew 28 they should be baptized "in the name of the Father and of the Son and of the Holy Spirit" (verse 19). If they had experienced that baptism, they would have heard of the Holy Spirit. It was then that Paul realized they were never baptized as believers in Jesus. Rather, they had only been baptized with the baptism of John. Paul continues:

"John indeed baptized with a baptism of repentance, saying to the people that they should believe on Him who would come after him, that is, on Christ Jesus."
Acts 19:4

Paul is telling them that John's baptism was a preparatory baptism. But now that Jesus had come, had died and had risen again, it was no longer sufficient.

When they heard this, they were baptized in the name of the Lord Jesus. And when Paul had laid his hands on them, the

*Holy Spirit came upon them, and they spoke with tongues and
prophesied.*
verses 5–6

Paul was thorough. He did not accept anything that was superficial. He wanted to make sure they were true believers in Jesus. They were baptized in water, and after they were baptized in water, Paul laid his hands upon them. Then, as a distinct experience, they were filled with the Holy Spirit and spoke in tongues and prophesied.

These verses set the limits to the baptism of John the Baptist. It did not lead people into a new birth experience and it was not sufficient to receive the Holy Spirit.

Study Questions

1. What special insights did you gain from this lesson?

   ----

2. Explain in your own words the difference between the baptism of John and the Christian baptism.

   ----

3. Derek Prince describes repentance as a way to prepare your heart for God. Would you agree with this definition? Describe in your own ways the purpose of repentance.

----

4. Consider the three elements of John's baptism: repentance, a public confession of sins and evidence of a changed life.

   * Do you think repentance is only needed once, or is it an ongoing process? Describe your own experiences.

   * How about confession of sins; do you think this is necessary or even helpful and why? Could it be beneficial to confess your sin to another person instead of to God alone? Have you ever confessed your sins to another person? Describe/discuss what happened.

----

5. John's baptism was meant to prepare Israel for the coming of the Messiah. Today, how can we prepare for the second coming of the Messiah?

----

6. Meditate on 1 John 1:9. Write down any thoughts that come from it. Take time to pray about it.

Pray for the Holy Spirit to clear up misunderstandings that you may have had concerning baptism and that you may grab its full significance in God's plan for you.

SUMMARY

- There are three main types of baptism mentioned in the Bible:
  - John's baptism
  - Christian baptism
  - Baptism in the Holy Spirit.

- The word baptize is taken directly from the Greek word baptizo and transliterated (represented in the letters of the English alphabet).

- To baptize has a very clear meaning in the original language which is to dip or to immerse– either by putting something down into water or by pouring water from above. Baptism is total, not partial.

- Baptism is a transition - out of one thing and into another. It is total immersion because we cannot just make a partial transition.

- In Mark 1:2-5, we learn about John's baptism and Scripture reveals two main purposes:
  - To prepare Israel for the coming of the Messiah. Messiah could not come until they were prepared and in our times, Messiah will not come again until we are prepared.
  - It was a dispensational link between law and grace. John's ministry was brief but important because he divided the history of God's people – he ended one period and initiated another. (Dispensationalism is an approach to biblical interpretation which states that God uses different means of working with people (Israel and the Church) during different periods of history, usually seven chronologically successive periods.)

SUMMARY

- In order to qualify for John's baptism, there were three chief requirements:
  - Repent - a change of mind and a resulting change of direction.
  - Public confession of sins. We don't always need to confess our sins publically, but only confessed sin qualifies for God's forgiveness.
  - Evidence of a changed life. (See Matt 3:7-8)

- While John's baptism was extremely important in preparing Israel for her Messiah and providing a link between two dispensations, it was limited in the following ways:
  - It did not produce the new birth. John was born of women but he was never "born again". He didn't enter into the new birth because that was not possible until Jesus came. (Matthew 11:11)
  - After the day of Pentecost when the Holy Spirit came in great power, it was no longer accepted as a substitute for Christian baptism. (Acts 19:1-5)

Once you have been
buried and raised again
in baptism, your life does
not belong to you.

Christian Baptism

Christian baptism covers what it means to be baptized as a believer in Jesus. I would have to say that this is far more important than the average Christian today realizes. Even the Baptists, who believe very strongly in the need for baptism, generally speaking, have very little understanding of the true significance and importance of being baptized in water.

Let me make it clear. First, you are not baptized into Jesus Christ because you are a sinner. This is not a baptism of repentance. We see this from Jesus' baptism.

> Then Jesus came from Galilee to John at the Jordan to be baptized by him. And John tried to prevent Him, saying, "I need to be baptized by You, and are You coming to me?"
> Matthew 3:13–14

At that moment, John did not know that Jesus was the Messiah. In the gospel of John it says that John the Baptist did not know Jesus until the Spirit of God descended upon Him and remained on Him. (See John 1:33–34.) That is a testimony to the life of Jesus. Even though John did not know He was the Messiah, he still said to Jesus: "You are more righteous than I am; I should not be the one to baptize You."

> But Jesus answered and said to him, "Permit it to be so now, for thus it is fitting for us to fulfill all righteousness." Then he allowed Him. When He had been baptized, Jesus came up

immediately from the water; and behold, the heavens were opened to Him, and He saw the Spirit of God descending like a dove and alighting upon Him. And suddenly a voice came from heaven, saying, "This is My beloved Son, in whom I am well pleased."
Matthew 3:15–17

In John's gospel it says the dove descended and remained upon Jesus (John 1:32). It is impossible to overemphasize the importance the New Testament attaches to being baptized in water. We see in this scene that all three persons of the Godhead endorsed it.

Jesus went through it, the Holy Spirit descended upon Him (and had not descended upon Him until He was baptized in water), and God the Father spoke from heaven saying, "This is My beloved Son, in whom I am well pleased." I say this with all reverence, but God bent over backwards to emphasize the extreme importance in His eyes of being baptized in water.

It is important to understand that Christian baptism is not a baptism of repentance, because Jesus had no sins of which to repent. Even though He was baptized by John, He was not baptized with John's baptism. What was the purpose? Jesus states it Himself:

"Permit it to be so now, for thus it is fitting for us to fulfill all righteousness."
Matthew 3:15

Jesus did not say, "It is fitting for Me to fulfill all righteousness," but "for us." He identifies Himself with all who will follow Him through the waters of baptism.

When He says, "It is fitting," He means it is appropriate or becoming to fulfill all righteousness in this way. When you are baptized in the name of Jesus Christ as a follower of Jesus, you are not baptized with a baptism of repentance. You have repented, but that is not why you are baptized. You are baptized to "fulfill all righteousness" or to "complete all righteousness."

This is such an important point that I want to emphasize it even more. In Romans 5:1, Paul writes of us, as believers in Jesus:

Therefore, having been justified by faith, we have peace with God through our Lord Jesus Christ.

Paul says that through our faith in Jesus we have been justified. "Justified" is one of the most important terms in the New Testament, but it is usually not well understood.

Justified has a number of different meanings: acquitted, declared not guilty, reckoned righteous, or made righteous.

Through our faith in Jesus, we have been acquitted, we are declared not guilty, we have been reckoned righteous and we have been made righteous.

That is why we should be baptized. Not because we have repented of our sins, but because it is the way to complete our righteousness. We already have righteousness imputed to us through our faith in Jesus. Water baptism is the appropriate way to fulfill, or complete, or carry out that righteousness.

Christian Baptism—A Commitment

Christian baptism is an identification with Jesus in His death, burial and resurrection. Paul states this in Romans:

Or do you not know that as many of us as were baptized into Christ Jesus were baptized into His death? Therefore, we were

buried with Him through baptism into death, that just as Christ
was raised from the dead by the glory of the Father, even so
we also should walk in newness of life.
Romans 6:3–4

We died with Christ Jesus. We are buried in the watery grave with Him. And then out of the watery grave we arise with Him to walk in newness of life—a different kind of life than we lived before.

When we are baptized, it signifies we have come to the end of our own life. We have come to the end of doing things in our own strength, righteousness and power. From now on, we are going to be identified with Jesus.

Romans 1:4 informs us that Jesus was raised from the dead by the Holy Spirit. When we come out of the watery tomb, it is to walk in the power of the Holy Spirit. Jesus did not raise Himself from the dead—that is very significant. He was raised from the dead by God the Father through the Holy Spirit.

[Jesus was] declared to be the Son of God with power
according to the Spirit of holiness, by the resurrection
from the dead.
Romans 1:4

Two different courts, one Jewish and one Roman, had sentenced Jesus to death as a criminal. But on the third day, when the tomb opened and He was raised from the dead, God reversed those decisions. He said, "This is My Son. He is altogether righteous. And I am bringing Him back to life because He is going to be the Author of life and godliness to all who will believe in Him."

How important the resurrection is! In water baptism, we are to act out in our own experience the reality of the resurrection.

Years ago, I was a teacher of African students training them to be teachers. As part of their training I told them, "People remember thirty percent of what they hear, sixty percent of what they hear and see, and ninety percent of what they hear, see and do. So don't let your pupils just listen to something. Get them involved in doing something that will indicate they understand the lesson." God follows the same principle. He does not just teach us in theory. He lets us see truths and He lets us then enact those truths. Water baptism is an enactment—a fresh enactment every time it takes place—of the death, burial and resurrection of Jesus Christ. In the early Church, new disciples could not get into the Church unless they went through that enactment of the faith they professed.

It wasn't enough just to say, "I believe." They had to act out their belief by being baptized.

Baptism—A Death Sentence

Once you have been buried and raised again in baptism, your life does not belong to you. If you want to go on living your own life, you should not be baptized, because baptism is your death sentence. But not only is it your death sentence; it then becomes your resurrection. When you are resurrected, your life no longer belongs to you. It belongs to the Lord. Baptism is your commitment to discipleship.

In Matthew 28:19–20, Jesus told His disciples what they were to do in proclaiming His gospel. He said:

> *"Go therefore and make disciples of all the nations, baptizing them in the name of the Father and of the Son and of the Holy Spirit, teaching them to observe all things that I have com manded you; and lo, I am with you always, even to the end of the age."*

Jesus said, "Go . . . and make disciples of all the nations." He never told us to make church members. The biggest problem in the Church today is church members who are not disciples. They actually misrepresent the truth that we are trying to proclaim. If you are not willing to be a disciple, you have no right to be baptized because it is a commitment to discipleship.

The disciples did not spend a lot of time teaching converts before they were baptized. But once the commitment was made, they taught them. When you stop to think about it, that pattern makes sense. Why waste time teaching uncommitted people? Let them prove their commitment in baptism and then begin to teach them what they need to know.

I saw this mistake in a mission in EastAfrica. The missionaries spent weeks teaching the candidates for baptism, but in the end they often baptized pagans! They had the head knowledge but they never had the heart experience. They had never made a real commitment to Jesus.

Requirements for Christian Baptism

Earlier we studied the requirements for John's baptism. We will now consider the requirements for Christian baptism.

The First Requirement

Jesus said, first of all, "Go and make disciples of all nations, baptizing them. . . ." A person who is to be baptized, then, must have heard the gospel of Jesus Christ and believed.

The gospel consists of just three historical facts: Jesus died, He was buried, and He rose again (1 Corinthians 15:1–4). If you believe that, it is reckoned to you as righteousness, and you are justified. We have no right to baptize people who have not been confronted by the simple facts of the gospel.

The Second Requirement

The second requirement is repentance. On the Day of Pentecost we read the response of Peter when the convicted, but unconverted, crowd said to him, "Men and brethren, what shall we do?" Peter's immediate answer was, "Repent." Remember that we discovered in a previous study that repentance is always the first step in any move toward God.

> *"Repent, and let every one of you be baptized in the name of Jesus Christ for the remission of sins; and you shall receive the gift of the Holy Spirit."*
> Acts 2:38

This is God's program all in one verse: repent, be baptized and receive the Holy Spirit. Why should we split it up and separate repentance from baptism by weeks or months?

When I was saved, I was so ignorant of the gospel that I just received the baptism in the Spirit at the same time. It did not happen in a church, but in an army barrack room. When I was baptized in the Holy Spirit, I received the gift of tongues and interpretation at the same time. Thank God, I had not yet been put together with Christians who said you have to wait to get all this.

Peter never indicated they needed to wait. He said, in effect, "It's a package deal: repent, be baptized in water, and receive the gift of the Holy Spirit." I know from experience that if you present the gospel to people the way Peter did and they respond, you will get the same results. It does not take a long time. It is not a long, drawn-out process. It is a crisis in a way. People are moving from one dimension to another dimension and it should be treated urgently.

The Third Requirement

Third, people have to believe to be baptized. In Mark 16:15–16 Jesus said to His disciples:

> *"Go into all the world and preach the gospel to every creature. He who believes and is baptized will be saved."*

You are not qualified to be baptized if you have not believed. "He who believes and is baptized will be saved."

Let me point out that Jesus never offers a guarantee of salvation to those who believe without being baptized. You may say, "I've settled this with the Lord." That is up to you. But you have no scriptural guarantee of salvation unless you have been baptized as a believer. And by "baptized," I mean your whole body right under the water and up again—total immersion.

The Fourth Requirement

The fourth condition is stated by Peter in 1 Peter 3:20–21. It is the answer to a good conscience toward God. In this passage Peter was writing about the days of Noah:

> *When once the Divine longsuffering* [or patience of God] *waited in the days of Noah, while the ark was being prepared, in which a few, that is, eight souls, were saved through water. - verse 20*

Peter said that God would not send the flood until the ark had been prepared. God was waiting patiently until the ark was ready. Only then would He release the flood. The account tells us that out of all the people on earth only eight were saved, which is a very solemn thought. Scholars have calculated that the population of the earth at the time of Noah was probably at least two million. Out of possibly two million people, only eight were saved.

Peter then continues:

There is also an antitype which now saves us—baptism (not the removal of the filth of the flesh, but the answer of a good conscience toward God). . . . - *verse 21*

The New King James translation which we use in this study says baptism is an "antitype." A "type" is a symbol or figure which represents an unseen spiritual fact. The "antitype" is the fulfillment of the type or the spiritual truth which it represented. Very simply, it means that baptism is the fulfillment of a symbol or figure from the Old Testament which, in this case, is the ark of Noah. Just as the ark saved Noah and his family from death, Peter is telling us that baptism saves us. It is not just having a bath to get clean.

We see, then, the fourth condition: you can answer God with a good conscience. In other words, you can say, "God, I know I was a sinner. I'm sorry. I repent. I believe Jesus died for me. I believe that through faith in Him I am justified, reckoned righteous. I've done all I can, Lord, in my condition as a sinner. Please accept me."

Having repented and believed, you answer to God with a good conscience in the act of baptism. You cannot do more than God asks. If you have done all that God asks, you have answered to God with a good conscience.

To recapitulate the four conditions for being baptized as a believer:
1. You must have heard the gospel.
2. You must have repented.
3. You must believe the gospel.
4. You must have a good conscience toward God.

I do not wish in any way to be controversial, but I think one fact is clear: an infant is incapable of fulfilling any of those four conditions. No one can deny it. It is a simple fact. I do not make this statement from any particular doctrinal persuasion, but I believe it is the clear testimony of Scripture.

MY NOTES

Study Questions

1. What special insights did you gain from this lesson?

   ----

2. Derek Prince explains the different reasons why it is important to be baptized in water. What reasons are there?

   ----

3. How does the Christian baptism differ from John's baptism? Are the requirements for Christian baptism different too?

---

4. Derek Prince describes at least two kinds of people that do not qualify for Christian baptism. Which ones? Would you agree with him?

---

5. Reflect/Discuss: "Once you have been buried and raised again, your life does not belong to you. If you want to go on living your own life you should not be baptized because baptism is your death sentence. What follows is your resurrection and when you are resurrected, your life does not belong to you." Share or write down your thoughts.

---

6. Assuming you have only a few minutes before you are to baptize a new convert, what instruction would you give in order for him to have the neccessary understanding to benefit fully from his experience of baptism? (For reference: Matthew 3:15, Acts 2:37-38, Mark 16:15, 1 Peter 3:21, Romans 6:1-7, Romans 6:11-14, Romans 6:3-4, Colossians 2:12, Romans 8:10)

7. Jesus said, "Go . . . and make disciples of all the nations." He never told us to make church members. What is the difference? What do you want to be?

8. If you wanted to respond to this study, what decision or step would you need to take today? Write it down. Pray about it. Act in faith.

SUMMARY

- When Jesus was baptized by John, He identified Himself with all who will follow Him through the waters of baptism.

- We are baptized in water, not because we have repented of our sins, but because it is the way to complete our righteousness that was imputed to us through our faith in Jesus. Water baptism is the appropriate way to fulfill, or complete, or carry out that righteousness.

- According to Romans 6:3, Christian baptism is identification with Jesus in His death, burial and resurrection. We died with Him, in the watery grave we are buried with Him, and then out of the watery grave we arise with Him to walk in newness of life.

- Anyone who is not willing to be a disciple, has no right to be baptized because it is a commitment to discipleship.

- Once you have been buried and raised again, your life does not belong to you but to Jesus.

- There are four requirements that we must fulfil before we can be baptized in water:
  - We need to hear the Gospel – Christ died for our sins, He was buried and He rose again on the third day (Matthew 28:19-20, 1 Corinthians 15:4)
  - Repentance – as the apostle Peter explained on the day of Pentecost. (Acts 2:38)
  - Faith or believe in Jesus. (Mark 16:15-16)
  - A good conscience towards God. (1 Peter 3:21)

- In Matthew 28:19-20, Jesus told us to go and make disciples, not church members.

MY NOTES

"He who believes and is
baptized will be saved"
(Mark 16:16).

Teaching for Baptism

Teaching for baptism need not take a long time. In a mission that I was once connected with, they would take six weeks to teach the converts and then baptize them. What they were doing many times was baptizing instructed pagans. The people had never really met the Lord, and their lives had never been changed.

Let's look at certain incidents in the book of Acts which speak about the length of time from conversion to baptism.

The Day of Pentecost

On the Day of Pentecost three thousand people were baptized the same day they heard the gospel message. The apostles did not say, "Now, we'll just wait. And if you bring forth fruit in six weeks, then we'll baptize you." Nor did they say, "When you've completed our new believer's class you've met our requirements for baptism."

They baptized them because they had met the right conditions: they had repented, believed, and they were willing to make a commitment. Notice, it was an unpopular commitment, because they were very much in the minority.

The Ethiopian Eunuch

In Acts 8 we read that Philip had just left a very exciting revival in Samaria and, because the angel sent him, he was on the road to Gaza. He had no idea why he was there, but he saw an Ethiopian eunuch in his chariot who was reading aloud from the prophet Isaiah. So Philip went near to him and asked, "Do you understand what you are reading?" (See Acts 8:30.)

He was reading this passage in Isaiah 53:7: "He was led as a sheep to the slaughter." The eunuch asked a very reasonable question in verse 34: "I ask you, of whom does the prophet say this, of himself or of some other man?" Acts 8:35 tells us:

> *Then Philip opened his mouth, and beginning at this Scripture, preached Jesus to him.*

Philip was an evangelist, and he is a pattern for all evangelists. His message was very simple, a one-word message: Jesus. In Samaria he preached "Christ" and on the road to Gaza he preached "Jesus."

I love the ministry of a true evangelist. I am not one myself, but every time I see a real evangelist in operation it is exciting. The evangelist's business is to introduce the sinner to the Savior; and having done that, his task is complete.

Philip introduced people to Christ in Samaria and moved on. A lot of people would have hung around because it was a very successful meeting. But Philip had instructions from God to move on and he did. That was a test of obedience.

To continue Philip's story:
> *Now as they went down the road, they came to some water. And the eunuch said, "See, here is water. What hinders me from being baptized?"... So he commanded the chariot to*

stand still. And both Philip and the eunuch went down into the
 water, and he [Philip] *baptized him* [the eunuch].
 verses 36, 38

The account only tells us that Philip preached "Jesus." But in the preaching of Jesus he must have said something about baptism because the eunuch took the initiative about baptism, not Philip. The eunuch said, "Here's water. Why shouldn't I be baptized right now?"

Philip replied, "All right, I'll do it." Then they both went down into the water. Please note that every time Christian baptism is described in the New Testament, the people go down into the water and come up out of the water.

Then Philip had an exciting experience. He was transported away by the Holy Spirit and the eunuch saw him no more. But the eunuch was not worried; he just went on his way rejoicing.

The point is, possibly only one or two hours had elapsed from the time the eunuch first heard the gospel until he was baptized. It was not a lengthy period of preparation. He met the requirements and was baptized.

The Household of Cornelius

In Acts 10 we read the story of the gospel being introduced to the Gentiles, which was a major transition for the Jewish disciples. Because of a vision from God, a Roman centurion had asked Peter to come to his house. Peter went very reluctantly to a Gentile home because it was against his religious convictions. He started to talk to them about Jesus and a wonderful thing happened. His sermon was interrupted. May God give us more interrupted sermons!

While Peter was still speaking these words, the Holy Spirit
 fell upon all those who heard the word. And those of the

circumcision who believed were astonished, as many as came
with Peter, because the gift of the Holy Spirit had been poured
out on the Gentiles also. For they heard them speak with
tongues and magnify God. Then Peter answered, "Can anyone
forbid water, that these should not be baptized who have r
eceived the Holy Spirit just as we have?" And he commanded
them to be baptized in the name of the Lord.
Acts 10:44–48

Notice, this Holy Spirit baptism is an immersion. They were immersed from above—a Niagara Falls immersion. Why were the disciples astonished? Because "they heard them speak with tongues and magnify God," which was a clear indication that the Gentiles had received the Holy Spirit as a sign of God's acceptance. No one could have been less ready to believe that Gentiles could become believers than Peter and his friends. But the moment they heard them speak with tongues they said, "This is it. They have received the same as we."

Then Peter commanded them to be baptized in water. He did not just make a recommendation. He commanded it. It was an act of obedience to God. It was perhaps an hour from the time they first spoke in tongues until they were baptized in water. There was no delay.

The Philippian Jailer

In Acts 16:22–40 we read that Paul and Silas had been thrown into prison in Philippi. They were in the innermost, maximum security jail at midnight, the darkest hour. And what were they doing? They were singing and praising the Lord! It says the other prisoners were listening to them—they never had people like Paul and Silas in that jail before.

At that particular point, their praises released the supernatural power of God and the whole jail was shaken to its foundations. Every door was opened and everybody's chains fell off. The jailer was about to commit suicide because, under the Roman system, if any prisoner escaped, he would have had to answer with his life for the prisoner. But Paul said, "Do yourself no harm, for we are all here." Verses 29–33 tell us:

> Then he [the jailer] *called for a light, ran in, and fell down trembling before Paul and Silas. And he brought them out and said, "Sirs, what must I do to be saved?" So they said, "Believe on the Lord Jesus Christ, and you will be saved, you and your household." Then they spoke the word of the Lord to him and all who were in his house. And he took them the same hour of the night and washed their stripes. And immediately he and all his family were baptized.*

Please note, "You and your household." As the head of his family, the jailer had the right to believe for his family. They were all of an age to hear the word of the Lord. They did not even wait for dawn—they were baptized immediately.

Water baptism for the Christians of the New Testament was an urgent matter. They did not wait for a baptismal service, because their complete salvation depended on it. "He who believes and is baptized will be saved" (Mark 16:16).

Spiritual Significance

The spiritual significance of baptism is stated in Romans 6.

> Or do you not know that as many of us as were baptized into Christ Jesus were baptized into His death? Therefore, we were buried with Him through baptism into death, that just as Christ was raised from the dead by the glory of the Father, even so we also should walk in newness of life.
> Romans 6:3–4

Every time Paul says, "Do you not know," I have observed that the majority of contemporary Christians do not know. It is remarkable.

In baptism we are identified with Jesus in death, in burial and, thank God, if we are buried with Him, we are also resurrected with Him.

Paul confirms this truth in the next verses:

> *For if we have been united together in the likeness of His death,*
> *certainly we also shall be in the likeness of His resurrection,*
> *knowing this, that our old man was crucified with Him, that*
> *the body of sin might be done away with, that we should no*
> *longer be slaves of sin.*
> *verses 5–6*

Paul is speaking about being buried in baptism. He says if we have been buried, then we can be assured we will be resurrected, as well. Baptism illustrates the fact that when Jesus died on the cross our sinful, carnal, rebellious nature was executed in Him. This is a revelation every Christian desperately needs.

You can have your sins forgiven and still be a rebel. A lot of people do just that. They go to church, confess their sins, receive forgiveness, and then they walk out and start sinning all over again. That is not God's purpose.

One reason why this happens is that they do not know the historical fact that when Jesus died on the cross, our old man—that rebel in every one of us—was executed. There is no other solution to the rebel; the only solution is execution. But the good news is the execution took place more than two thousand years ago when Jesus died on the cross.

The Process of Reckoning

In verse 11 Paul applies this fact:

Likewise you also, reckon yourselves to be dead indeed to sin, but alive to God in Christ Jesus our Lord. - verse 11

Paul says, "You know it. Then you have to reckon it." You have to reckon that you are dead to sin but alive to God. "Reckon" means to count it as a completed fact. The outward process of that reckoning is water baptism. You go down into the grave and come up out of the grave. You leave your old sinful nature behind in the grave and you come out a new creature.

There is one other important passage concerning this in Colossians 2. Paul is writing to Christians and he says:

In Him you were also circumcised with the circumcision made without hands, by putting off the body of the sins of the flesh, by the circumcision of Christ.
Colossians 2:11

Under the Jewish law, circumcision was simply removing a small portion of flesh. But Christian circumcision is putting off the whole sinful, fleshly nature—the whole body.

When a body has died, what is the next thing we need to do? Bury it! It is offensive to leave a dead body lying around unburied. When I was with the British forces in North Africa during World War II, we never left a corpse on the ground; we always put it underground. If you have died, don't lie around unburied. Get buried in water baptism so you can enjoy your resurrection!

Paul goes on in Colossians 2, that after having put off the body of the flesh we must be:

buried with Him in baptism, in which you also were raised with Him through faith in the working of God, who raised Him from the dead.   verse 12

Baptism only works for those who believe. It is through our faith in what God will do that we are raised. If we do not believe, it does not work. This is why Paul says in Romans that we must "reckon."

Faith, as we have studied, is believing something is true even if you cannot see or feel it. It is our faith in "the working of God" that will make it real in our experience.

Facts about Christian Baptism

We will now consider certain important facts about Christian baptism. First, in Galatians 3:

For as many of you as were baptized into Christ have put on Christ. - verse 27

We are baptized into Christ. We are not baptized into a denomination or a church. This is a serious error which is prevalent in many portions of Christianity today.

Again, I go back to my days in East Africa. The largest evangelical mission there would not accept anybody as a member who had not been baptized into their mission. A person might have been validly baptized as a believer, but if it was not in that mission they had to be baptized again. That is an error; it is fleshly human religion pretending to be spiritual.

We are not baptized into a church. Thank God, we are baptized into Christ; and it is effective only through faith. In our faith we need to understand that our new life is empowered by the Holy Spirit—faith in the "working of God." The same Spirit that raised Jesus from the dead also works in us.

Examples from the Old Testament

The first picture from the Old Testament is one we have already looked at in 1 Peter 3: it is Noah's ark. Peter says the antitype to Noah's ark is baptism in water.

The message of Noah's ark is, first of all, that judgment was coming. There was only one way of escape from judgment and that was in the ark. The flood represents God's judgment. The ark is a picture of Jesus Christ. In the ark you can pass safely through the waters of judgment. Outside of the ark you will be drowned. There is no other way of escape but to be in the ark, Jesus Christ. In the ark you pass through the water in safety, and you come out into a totally different new life. The old life has been washed away, a new life has opened up to you. That is the picture of Noah's ark.

The second picture is found in 1 Corinthians:

> Moreover, brethren, I do not want you to be unaware that all our fathers were under the cloud, all passed through the sea, all were baptized into Moses in the cloud and in the sea. . . . These things became our examples [or patterns].
> 1 Corinthians 10:1–2, 6

Paul is telling us that every Israelite in the exodus (the deliverance from Egypt), passed through two experiences. The cloud came down over them from above, and thus they were baptized in the cloud. They also went down into the water of the Red Sea, passing through the water, and came up out of the water. Therefore Paul says they were baptized in the sea.

Here we see this double baptism that is appointed for every believer. The cloud comes down on you from above and you are immersed in the cloud. Then you go down into the water, pass through the water, and come up out of the water. When the Israelites came up out of the water, they started a new life with new laws and a new leader. Everything else was left behind.

Notice that it was the water that cut off the Egyptians. We need to understand that although the Israelites had been saved in Egypt by faith in the blood of the lamb, that experience in itself did not separate them from the Egyptians. It was the water that separated them.

In like manner, it is baptism that separates us from the power and authority of our old lives. We can believe in the blood of Jesus and be saved. But we are not separated until we are baptized.

Release from the Old Life

I have encountered literally thousands of people who were delivered from evil spirits. Wherever possible, I always tell them, "If you want to keep your deliverance, be baptized in water." Baptism in water is the cutoff from the power of the old life. The blood saves you in Egypt but the water separates you from Egypt. The Israelites were separated by the water and by the cloud.

It says they were baptized "into Moses" (1 Corinthians 10:2). In other words, this brought them under the leadership of Moses. We, on the other hand, are not baptized into Moses, but we are baptized into Christ. Christ becomes our leader. But in order to enter into Him in the scriptural way, we have to pass under the cloud and we have to pass through the water. This is such a vivid picture of the power of baptism.

The Element of Faith

In Hebrews we are told that this baptism was only by faith.

> By faith they passed through the Red Sea as by dry land,
> whereas the Egyptians, attempting to do so, were drowned.
> Hebrews 11:29

If you are baptized as an unbeliever, you will go down into the water a dry sinner and come up a wet sinner! That is the only change that takes place.

I once heard the testimony of a man who was a church soloist. In order to sing in the church, the leadership required their singers to be baptized. He agreed to this. There he was, a dry sinner; he went down into the water and came up a wet sinner. That is all that happened because there was no faith involved. (Later on, when he received Jesus he was re-baptized.)

How did all Israel pass through the Red Sea? By faith. The Egyptians were drowned because they had no faith. So, if you are baptized in water but you are not a believer, all that happens is you will get wet. You can only pass through to the newness of life by faith in Jesus.

An Urgent Matter

The urgency of baptism is a very serious subject, much more serious than most denominations and churches recognize today. Many times people will become convicted and will ask, "What comes next?"

I say, "Be baptized." "When?"

"As soon as possible. Now!"

When I lived in Florida, there were times when someone had just met the Lord and I took them down to the ocean for baptism. They later had to drive home, sometimes a long distance, and with no change of clothes. But they were so determined they said, "That's all right; we'll go home wet!" They saw the importance and the urgency of baptism.

We need to have a reorientation in the Church about our thinking regarding baptism. It is part of complete salvation. I am not saying that if anyone, as a believer, is not baptized that they will not be saved. That is between them and the Lord. But I have no authority to tell them that they will be saved either. Jesus said, "He who believes and is baptized will be saved" (Mark 16:16).

It is my heartfelt desire that as you read this booklet, you will stop and allow the Holy Spirit to speak to you individually about the importance of receiving water baptism.

If you were baptized as an unbeliever as part of a church ritual, or if you feel convicted by the Holy Spirit that you need to receive baptism again in order to fully apprehend by faith its true importance, then I would urge you to seek out someone who can baptize you with a full understanding of its spiritual significance.

If, however, you believe you have received a water baptism as I have described it from the Scriptures, then make it your regular exercise to reckon yourself by faith to be dead, buried and resurrected with Christ Jesus, walking in "newness of life."

Let me close this booklet with a personal prayer for you.

Lord Jesus Christ, You are Head over all things to the Church, which is Your body. I bring to You this individual who is reading this booklet. Only You know exactly in what relationship they are to You.

Lord, if this individual really is saved and wants to become a disciple but has not yet been baptized in water, I pray earnestly that You will put an urgency in this person's heart by the Holy Spirit to take that necessary step of obedience.

Lord Jesus, may this be for Your glory and for the building up of Your body. In Your name I pray.

Amen.

Study Questions

1. What special insights did you gain from this lesson?

   ....

   ....

   ....

   ....

2. Why are each of the conditions for baptism important for the believer to experience before baptism?

   ....

   ....

   ....

   ....

3. Would you feel confident to lead a new convert into Christian baptism? Why / why not?

----

4. In 1 Corinthians 10:1-2, Paul compares the Christian baptism with the moment God delivered the Israelites from Egypt. Read the story in Exodus 12:21-36 and 14:5-31. How did they show their faith? What was it, that cut off the Egyptians?

----

5. At this point, you find yourself in one of two positions: either you have fulfilled the conditions of hearing the gospel, repentance from dead works, faith toward God and the answer of a good conscience and have been baptised in water and into Christ or you have not. As such, it is appropriate to have two possible responses.

    If you still need to be baptised, then here is a suggested prayer:

Heavenly Father, I thank You that the eyes of my heart have been enlightened (Ephesians 1:18) to see the great significance of water baptism in the life of a believer. I have come to appreciate the need to fulfil this requirement without delay and that there is no guarantee of salvation without baptism as Mark 16:16 tells me that "he who believes and is baptized will be saved."

I pray that You would lead me to a mature Christian who can baptise me as a matter of urgency in the name of the Father and of the Son and of the Holy Spirit in accordance with Matthew 28:19.

In Jesus' name I pray. Amen

If you have fulfilled the conditions as presented in Scripture and have been baptised in water, here is a suggested prayer:

Heavenly Father, I thank you for this wonderful reminder of what you have done for me through baptism as I have been identified with Jesus in His death, burial and resurrection.

I ask that you would help me to share this truth with many other people so that they too can find the freedom that I have found through this simple, yet imperative, enactment of faith in the Gospel.

In Jesus' name I pray. Amen

SUMMARY

- Teaching and preparation for baptism need not take a long time. In the examples of the day of Pentecost, the Ethiopian eunuch, the household of Cornelius and that of the Philippian jailer all had an urgency about them.

- The spiritual significance of baptism is three-fold: it indicates our identification with Jesus Christ in His death, burial and resurrection (Romans 6:3-11).

- Baptism only works for those who have faith in the working of God– if we don't believe, it doesn't work (Colossians 2:12).

- After being baptized, we live a new life through Jesus Christ and for Him. This new life is empowered by the Holy Spirit. The same power that raised Christ from the dead also works in us (Romans 8:11).

- Noah's ark is an antitype of baptism. Judgement was coming and the only way of escape was in the ark. The ark represents Jesus Christ. In the ark you can pass safely through the waters of judgment but outside of it you will be submerged (1 Peter 3:20-21).

In the next study, *Immersion in the Holy Spirit*, you will continue the study of the doctrine of baptisms by examining the third New Testament baptism, the baptism in the Holy Spirit.

*Recall and write down the verses you memorized
at the beginning of this book:*

Romans 6:3

Romans 6:4

About the Author

Derek Prince (1915–2003) was born in India of British parents. He was educated as a scholar of Greek and Latin at Eton College and King's College, Cambridge in England. Upon graduation he held a fellowship (equivalent to a professorship) in Ancient and Modern Philosophy at King's College. Prince also studied Hebrew, Aramaic, and modern languages at Cambridge and the Hebrew University in Jerusalem. As a student, he was a philosopher and self-proclaimed agnostic.

Bible Teacher

While in the British Medical Corps during World War II, Prince began to study the Bible as a philosophical work. Converted through a powerful encounter with Jesus Christ, he was baptized in the Holy Spirit a few days later. Out of this encounter, he formed two conclusions: first, that Jesus Christ is alive; second, that the Bible is a true, relevant, up-to-date book. These conclusions altered the whole course of his life, which he then devoted to studying and teaching the Bible as the Word of God.

Discharged from the army in Jerusalem in 1945, he married Lydia Christensen, founder of a children's home there. Upon their marriage, he immediately became father to Lydia's eight adopted daughters – six Jewish, one Palestinian Arab, and one English. Together, the family saw the rebirth of the state of Israel in 1948. In the late 1950s, they adopted another daughter while Prince was serving as principal of a teacher training college in Kenya.

In 1963, the Princes immigrated to the United States and pastored a church in Seattle. In 1973, Prince became one of the founders of Intercessors for America. His book Shaping History through Prayer and

Fasting has awakened Christians around the world to their responsibility to pray for their governments. Many consider underground translations of the book as instrumental in the fall of communist regimes in the USSR, East Germany, and Czechoslovakia.

Lydia Prince died in 1975, and Prince married Ruth Baker (a single mother to three adopted children) in 1978. He met his second wife, like his first wife, while she was serving the Lord in Jerusalem. Ruth died in December 1998 in Jerusalem, where they had lived since 1981.

Teaching, Preaching and Broadcasting

Until a few years before his own death in 2003 at the age of eighty-eight, Prince persisted in the ministry God had called him to as he traveled the world, imparting God's revealed truth, praying for the sick and afflicted, and sharing his prophetic insights into world events in the light of Scripture. Internationally recognized as a Bible scholar and spiritual patriarch, Derek Prince established a teaching ministry that spanned six continents and more than sixty years.

He is the author of more than fifty books, six hundred audio teachings, and one hundred video teachings, many of which have been translated and published in more than one hundred languages.

He pioneered teaching on such groundbreaking themes as generational curses, the biblical significance of Israel, and demonology. Prince's radio program, which began in 1979, has been translated into more than a dozen languages and continues to touch lives. Derek's main gift of explaining the Bible and its teaching in a clear and simple way has helped build a foundation of faith in millions of lives. His nondenominational, nonsectarian approach has made his teaching equally relevant and helpful to people from all racial and religious backgrounds, and his teaching is estimated to have reached more than half the globe.

DPM Worldwide Ministry

In 2002, he said, "It is my desire – and I believe the Lord's desire – that this ministry continue the work, which God began through me over sixty years ago, until Jesus returns." Derek Prince Ministries International continues to reach out to believers in over 140 countries with Derek's teaching, fulfilling the mandate to keep on "until Jesus returns." This is accomplished through the outreaches of more than thirty Derek Prince offices around the world, including primary work in Australia, Canada, China, France, Germany, the Netherlands, New Zealand, Norway, Russia, South Africa, Switzerland, the United Kingdom, and the United States.

For current information about these and other worldwide locations, visit **www.derekprince.com.**

FOUNDATIONS
faith life essentials

www.dpmuk.org/shop

This book is part of a series of 10 studies on the foundations of the Christian faith.

Order the other books to get everything you need to develop a strong, balanced, Spirit-filled life!

1. Founded on the Rock

There is only one foundation strong enough for the Christian life, and we must be sure our lives are built on Jesus Himself.

2. Authority and Power of God's Word

Both the Bible and Jesus Christ are identified as the Word of God. Learn how Jesus endorsed the authority of Scripture and how to use God's Word as a two-edged sword yourself.

3. Through Repentance to Faith

What is faith? And how can you develop it? It starts with repentance: to change the way we think and to begin acting accordingly.

4. Faith and Works

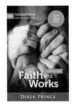

Many Christians live in a kind of twilight - halfway between law and grace. They do not know which is which nor how to avail themselves of God's grace.

5. The Doctrine of Baptisms

A baptism is a transition - out of an old way of living into a totally new way of living. All of our being is involved. This study explains the baptism of John and the Christian (water) baptism. The baptism in the Holy Spirit is explained in 'Immersion in the Spirit'.

6. Immersion in the Spirit

Immersion can be accomplished in two ways: the swimming pool way and the Niagara Falls way. This book takes a closer look at the Niagara Falls experience, which relates to the baptism of the Holy Spirit.

7. Transmitting God's Power

Laying on of hands is one of the basic tenets of the Christian faith. By it, we may transmit God's blessing and authority and commission someone for service. Discover this Biblical doctrine!

8. At The End of Time

In this study, Derek Prince reveals the nature of eternity and outlines what lies ahead in the realm of end-time events.

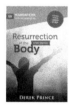

9. Resurrection of the Body

The death and resurrection of Jesus produced a change in the universe. Derek explains here how the resurrection of Jesus impacted man's spirit, soul, and body.

10. Final Judgment

This book examines the four major, successive scenes of judgment in eternity. Exploring the distinctive aspects of these four judgments, Derek opens the Scriptures to bring forth treasures hidden there.

Christian Foundations Course

If you have enjoyed this study and would like to deepen your knowledge of God's Word and apply the teaching – why not enrol on Derek Prince's Christian Foundations Bible Course?

Building on the Foundations of God's Word

A detailed study of the six essential doctrines of Christianity found in Hebrews 6:1-2.

- Scripture-based curriculum
- Practical, personal application
- Systematic Scripture memorisation
- Opportunity for questions and personal feedback from course tutor
- Certificate upon completion
- Modular based syllabus
- Set your own pace
- Affordable
- Based on *Foundational Truths for Christian Living.*

For a prospectus, application form and pricing information, please visit www.dpmuk.org, call 01462 492100 or send an e-mail to enquiries@dpmuk.org

Foundational Truths For Christian Living

Develop a strong, balanced, Spirit-filled life, by discovering the foundations of faith: salvation; baptism, the Holy Spirit, laying on hands, the believers' resurrection and eternal judgment.

Its reader-friendly format includes a comprehensive index of topics and a complete index of Scripture verses used in the book.

ISBN 978-1-908594-82-2
Paperback and eBook
£ 13.99

www.dpmuk.org/shop

More best-sellers by Derek Prince

- Blessing or Curse: You can Choose
- Bought with Blood
- Life-Changing Spiritual Power
- Marriage Covenant
- Prayers & Proclamations
- Self-Study Bible Course
- Shaping History Through Prayer and Fasting
- Spiritual Warfare for the End Times
- They Shall Expel Demons
- Who is the Holy Spirit?

For more titles: www.dpmuk.org/shop

Inspired by Derek's teaching?

Help make it available to others!

If you have been inspired and blessed by this Derek Prince resource you can help make it available to a spiritually hungry believer in other countries, such as China, the Middle East, India, Africa or Russia.

Even a small gift from you will ensure that that a pastor, Bible college student or a believer elsewhere in the world receives a free copy of a Derek Prince resource in their own language.

Donate now: www.dpmuk.org/give
or visit www.derekprince.com

Derek Prince Ministries

DPM–Asia/Pacific
38 Hawdon Street
Sydenham
Christchurch 8023
New Zealand
T: + 64 3 366 4443
E: admin@dpm.co.nz
W: www.dpm.co.nz

DPM–Australia
15 Park Road
Seven Hills
New South Wales 2147
Australia
T: +61 2 9838 7778
E: enquiries@au.derekprince.com
W: www.derekprince.com.au

DPM–Canada
P. O. Box 8354
Halifax
Nova Scotia B3K 5M1
Canada
T: + 1 902 443 9577
E: enquiries.dpm@eastlink.ca
W: www.derekprince.org

DPM–France
B.P. 31, Route d'Oupia
34210 Olonzac
France
T: + 33 468 913872
E: info@derekprince.fr
W: www.derekprince.fr

DPM–Germany
Söldenhofstr. 10
83308 Trostberg
Germany
T: + 49 8621 64146
E: ibl@ibl-dpm.net
W: www.ibl-dpm.net

DPM-Netherlands
Nijverheidsweg 12
7005 BJ, Doetinchem
Netherlands
T: +31 251-255044
E: info@derekprince.nl
W: www.derekprince.nl

Offices Worldwide

DPM–Norway
P. O. Box 129
Lodderfjord
N-5881 Bergen
Norway
T: +47 928 39855
E: xpress@dpskandinavia.com
W: www.derekprince.no

Derek Prince Publications Pte. Ltd.
P. O. Box 2046
Robinson Road Post Office
Singapore 904046
T: + 65 6392 1812
E: dpmchina@singnet.com.sg
W: www.dpmchina.org (English)
      www.ygmweb.org (Chinese)

DPM–South Africa
P. O. Box 33367
Glenstantia
0010 Pretoria
South Africa
T: +27 12 348 9537
E: enquiries@derekprince.co.za
W: www.derekprince.co.za

DPM–Switzerland
Alpenblick 8
CH-8934 Knonau
Switzerland
T: + 41 44 768 25 06
E: dpm-ch@ibl-dpm.net
W: www.ibl-dpm.net

DPM–UK
PO Box 393
Hitchin SG5 9EU
United Kingdom
T: + 44 1462 492100
E: enquiries@dpmuk.org
W: www.dpmuk.org

DPM–USA
P. O. Box 19501
Charlotte NC 28219
USA
T: + 1 704 357 3556
E: ContactUs@derekprince.org
W: www.derekprince.org

Lightning Source UK Ltd.
Milton Keynes UK
UKHW021657130720
366461UK00005B/142

9 781782 635451